Serenity Prayer

Adult Coloring Book

The Complete text of the Serenity Prayer in Large, Simple Coloring Font with 14 Mandala Coloring Pages

AGNES BARTOCCELLI

ESTHER PINCINI

Serenity Prayer Adult Coloring Book
The Complete text of the Serenity Prayer in Large, Simple Coloring Font
with 14 Mandala Coloring Pages

by Agnes Bartoccelli and Esther Pincini

Contains the full text of the original "Serenity Prayer"
written by Reinhold Niebuhr (1892-1971)

Creative Content Copyright © Magdalene Press 2016

ISBN 978-1-77335-087-5

Magdalene Press, 2016

God grant

me the

serenity

To accept

the things

I cannot

change;

Courage to change the things I can;

And
wisdom to
know the
difference.

Living
one day
at a time;

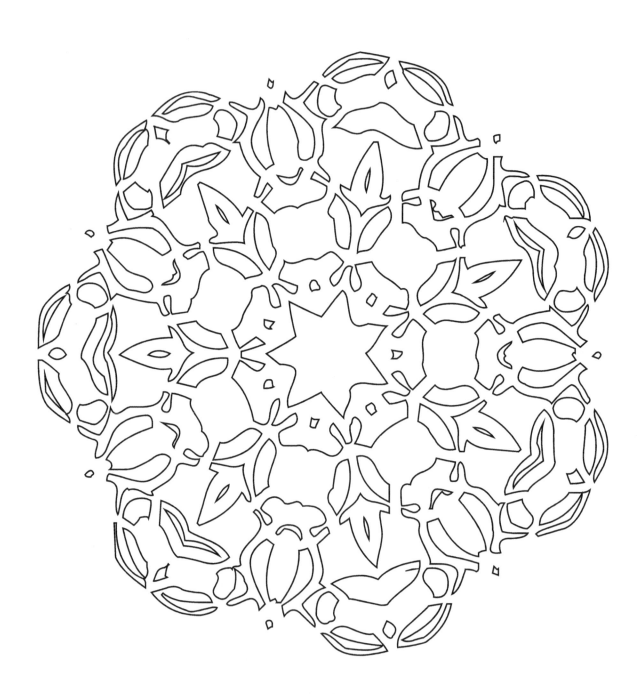

Enjoying

one moment

at a time;

Accepting hardships as the pathway to peace;

Taking, as
He did, this
sinful world

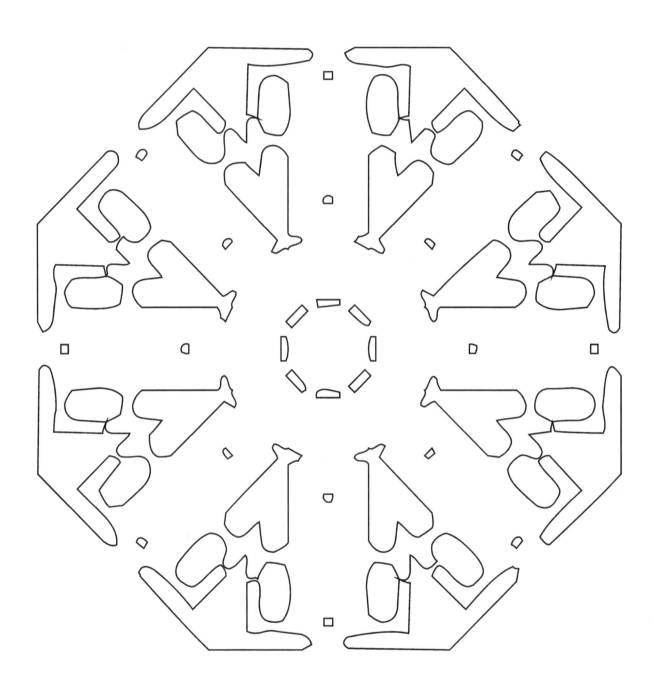

As it is,
not as I
would have
it;

Trusting that He will make all things right

 f I

surrender

to His Will;

So that I may be reasonably happy in this life

And

supremely

happy with

Him

Forever

and ever in

the next.